40 Problems ... 41 Prayers

40 $\mathcal{P}$ROBLEMS ...

Difficult Situations Women Experience

... 41 $\mathcal{P}$RAYERS

Words of Wisdom to Help Ease You Through

Nancy J. Bremer

NANCY J. BREMER

40 PROBLEMS ... 41 PRAYERS
Copyright © 2008 Nancy J. Bremer

ISBN 978-1-886068-21-6
Library of Congress Control Number: 2008929420
Personal Growth • Christian Life

Published by Fruitbearer Publishing, L.L.C.
P.O. Box 777, Georgetown, DE 19947
(302) 856-6649 • FAX (302) 856-7742
www.fruitbearer.com • fruitbearer.publishing@verizon.net

All Scripture quotations, unless otherwise indicated, are taken from the *NEW INTERNATIONAL VERSION®, NIV®*, Copyright © 1973, 1978, 1984 International Bible Society. Used by permission of Zondervan Bible Publishers. All rights reserved.

Scripture quotations marked KJV are taken from the *The King James Version of the Holy Bible (KJV)*, public domain.

Printed by
Bethany Press International
6820 West 115th Street
Bloomington, MN 55438
www.bethanypress.com

Special Thanks:

To Bobbie Lybrand, William Craig III, and Peggy M. White—my three biggest "cheerleaders."

Special thanks, too, to Pat Peterson for her encouragement and support.

Contents

Introduction 9

What is God's Plan for Me 12

Your First Heartbreak 14

I Want a Child, My Husband Doesn't 16

Intimacy after the Birth of a Child 18

Having a
    Developmentally Challenged Child 20

The Loss of a Child through Adoption 22

An Argument with your Child 24

Dealing with a Teenage Child 26

Dealing with Drugs 28

A Missing Child 30

A Full Plate 32

Drunk Drivers 34

Illness of an Adult Child 38

Being an Alcoholic 40

Budget Problems 42

Cleaning Out the Closet 44

I Have an Attitude 46

Menopause 48

Being Diagnosed with Cancer 50

Dealing with Aging 52

How do Hobbies become so Political 54

Not being Selected for a Certain Job 56

You don't Like your Job 58

Frustration with Co-workers 60

When a Consultant is Hired to Do Your Job .62

The Loss of a Job 64

My Water Pipes Broke 66

My House Burned Down (or Up) 68

The Loss of a Friend
    due to Changes in Lifestyles 70

The Loss of a Friend
    through Death from Illness 72

Suicide 74

An Abusive Relationship 76

Disappearance of a Spouse 78

The Loss of a Spouse
    through Divorce (no children) 80

The Loss of a Spouse through Death 82

Death of Parents 84

Living Alone 86

Spending Christmas Alone 88

Hip Replacement 90

Living In a Retirement Community 92

Introduction

For all the books of prayer for women, the intention of *Forty Problems ... Forty-One Prayers* is to be different. The prayers address difficult situations women experience in their lives. In the whole scheme of things, forty one is actually smaller than the tip of the iceberg.

There are more prayers than problems, because there are two prayers for drunk drivers—one that addresses a personal loss and one that addresses the loss of a loved one.

Women are fascinating creatures (but we knew that). When I started this book, I asked several women to send me information on difficult experiences they had faced and to tell me how they felt, what occurred, and what the outcome was. Some of them did send me overviews of experiences they had dealt with and overcome. Many, however, said that they couldn't think of anything. I looked at the answers of many of these women and thought, "I can think of several things you have survived!" That's one reason women are so amazing. They overcome obstacles and move on with their lives, leaving behind any feelings of having had a difficult time. I was impressed. However, we do encounter difficult times in our lives, and our emotions run the whole gamut of the spectrum.

I hope that these prayers touch your heart and ease some of the strain you may be encountering in your lives. Use them as you need them, and share them with others who may need them.

For those women who sent me information, I offer my thanks and gratitude. They provided such interesting information on a wonderful array of difficult situations and a good starting point for my writing.

Nancy J. Bremer

40 Problems ... 41 Prayers

What is God's Plan for Me?

Most women will, at some point in their lives, ask God what they are meant to do with their life. Some ask at a very young age, some when they are older or when life experiences start to get overwhelming, some when they are old or ill. The question is always sincere and the quest for the answer may seem daunting. It may seem that they are so burdened or laden with problems that they can't even begin to wonder what God's plan is. What do they go through and how do they keep going?

Lord, my life feels like it's a mess. I'm a mess. It seems that every time I turn around there is another crisis in my life. Some are major and some are minor, but there is always a crisis. My mother is ill, my daughter is trying to find herself, my nephew is in an accident, my husband and I have split up, my job is not what I want to do. It is always something.

What is amazing is that while I am in constant turmoil where I feel that every aspect of my life is in "crisis mode," my friends are asking me for help to solve their problems! I can't even figure out my own! I feel flattered. I will talk with them, and most importantly, I will listen to them. I worry that I may mislead them and I wonder if just being there for them is part of your plan for my life.

Help me to help myself and others. Guide me on the path to fulfill the plans you have for me. Let me reach out to you and step out to get the skills necessary to excel at your plan for my life. Let me grow in confidence so I can feel worthy, and so I can lift others up through faith and in faith. Lead me to do the things I need to do for myself, my friends, and my family. Let me always remember that you are with me and will support me in whatever life brings my way. In addition, let me share that confidence with everyone I meet. Amen.

Your First Heartbreak

The age at which a female suffers her first heart-break can vary from early childhood, to the teenage years, to being a young adult, or as a more mature woman. Whenever it occurs, it is devastating. There are myriads of tears and lamentations. There is a degree of guilt, and a portion of anger. The majority of women survive. Perhaps the following prayer would help cope with this life occurrence.

Lord, I am devastated by this loss. I don't understand why this has happened to me. I am a good person and I loved [this person] with my whole heart. It hurts. Help me recover and move on with my life. Through faith, provide the balm that is needed to soothe the pain. Let me look at what was good and how it has helped me grow as an individual. Let me remember the happy times, and not dwell on the sad times. I was cared for and loved during this relationship; so I am worthy of caring and love. May I find someone who sees the good qualities in me and wants to share their life (or at least a part of it) with me. Let this person allow me to love them—maybe even with my whole heart. Heal my heart, let me look for the good, and send me someone special to love. Amen.

I Want a Child, My Husband Doesn't

What do you do when you really want a child and your husband really doesn't? How do you cope with this huge difference in thinking and the effect it will have on your entire life? How do you come to terms with this fact, and how do you maintain your relationship with the man you married?

Lord, help me. My heart is broken and my cheeks are streaked with tears. I want to have a child, and my husband has said that he does not. How could this have happened? I thought we wanted the same things in life. Now I feel like I am going in one direction and he is going in another direction. This is not good for our relationship or our marriage, and I can feel the animosity building on both sides.

Please give me patience and perseverance. Show me how to talk with him in a non-threatening manner and try to understand what his fears are about having a child. May we talk this through and determine if we can find a solution to his fears. Enable me to love him enough to listen and to ask for clarification so that I can truly understand what he is feeling and thinking. If we are meant to have a child, please, please let it be. If we are not, please guide me so that I can find out if I am supposed to have a child or even if I am supposed to be in this relationship. Let us seek the counseling we will need to get through this. Please may he be open to talking with another person and may I be open enough to accept what a counselor recommends. All this I pray in your name. Amen.

Intimacy after the Birth of a Child

Often after the birth of a child, a woman loses interest in intimacy with her husband/partner. There is post-partum depression, lack of sleep, and the newness of being totally responsible for taking care of every aspect of this little person's life. It can be overwhelming and exhausting. There are so many additional tasks to be done, and those in addition to all the other tasks that have always needed to be done. By the end of the day, you are just plain tired. Then you have the issue of interrupted sleep from getting up at least once, if not more, during the night to feed this baby. Where is the energy and excitement going to come from to enjoy an intimate relationship?

Lord, I am so tired. This baby is just wearing me out. I love this child, but he/she is draining all my energy. There is so much to do with feeding, changing, rocking, and doing laundry, not to mention all the other chores that have to be done around the house. I am trying to show my husband/partner how much I love him. I go to great efforts to keep the house clean and the clothes washed, and I strive to have a nice dinner prepared each evening. It can get really tough if the baby's schedule interrupts my efforts. By the time I put the baby down for the night (or at least a couple of hours) I am ready for bed myself. That does not include intimacy. I just do not have the energy. I love my husband/partner, but I am not interested in sex. Am I an awful person?

Please help me grow into this dual role of mother and wife/partner. Let me be sure that my husband/partner knows how much I love him and does not feel that all of my love and loving feelings are going to this child. May we learn to work as a team in taking care of all the things that need to be done. Teach us to make time for one another, time that is not interrupted by the needs and wants of a child. We need to create a calendar to make sure that we have the time and the intimacy that we need to ensure that our relationship remains loving and strong, and that there are no feelings of jealousy or resentment. As we get more comfortable with taking care of this child, may these times together grow stronger and more frequent, knowing that the needs of all of us are being tended to. This I pray in your name. Amen.

Having a Developmentally Challenged Child

Many, many children with developmental difficulties are born to mothers of all ages. The child may be slower to learn, or have Spina Bifida or Down's Syndrome, or any other of a myriad of problems. For all the difficulties these children face, what do the mothers face, and how do they feel?

✝ Lord, my child is developmentally chal-
lenged. I worry so. Not just for now,
although I constantly worry now, but also for the
future. What will it bring to this child and to me?
How can I deal with this problem that is so heavy on
my heart and still ensure that this child has every
opportunity to do everything possible with his/her
life? There are many days of (surgery/therapy/doctor
visits/etc.). Where will the money from? Who will
help me to help this child of mine?

Please shine your grace down on me and calm
my fears. Through faith, let me build a strength that
will carry me through all that lies ahead for both my
child and me. Let me always believe in this child just
as you always believe in me. For every tear I shed let
there be a smile for every small accomplishment this
child achieves. Let me always remember that we are
all here for a reason and that no matter how many
trials and tribulations my child and I must face, it is
being done for you—and possibly for the betterment
of others. Let those children who have come before
my child leave a legacy of better treatment, more
advanced technology, and more hope. And let my
child leave the same legacy for those children who
will follow. This I pray in your name. Amen.

The Loss of a Child through Adoption

Although many children are born into single parent families and raised by their birth mother (or perhaps father), many women will or have experienced the process of giving a child up for adoption. It is a decision that presents the birth mother with a major emotional struggle, and can be a cause of major turmoil within the family or the man/woman relationship. The bond between the mother and the unborn child is very strong and much thought and anguish is experienced in deciding the best way to deal with the pregnancy and the unborn child. How does the mother feel after the adoption is final?

Lord, my heart is so heavy. I have literally lost a part of myself. I have given this child up for adoption so that he/she has every chance for a full and better life, one that I am not able to provide. I wanted to keep this child, but I didn't have the resources or support I needed. Even though I know this is best for the child, it is taking a terrible toll on me. I am a mess. I cry. I mourn this loss. I find it difficult to get motivated and move on with my life. This was my child. I may or may not have other children, but this was my child!

Please keep this child safe and cared for and loved beyond measure. May he/she grow and learn and make something wonderful of his/her life. I will keep this child in my heart all of my life. I will remember each birthday and I may cry a tear or two on Mother's Day. I know that I will survive this loss. I know that you have a plan, not just for my life, but for the life of this child. No child is an accident. I pray that you will be with both of us. May we both look to you in faith to do what it is you have gifted us to do. And if it is in the plan, let us be reunited one day. Amen.

An Argument with your Child

At one time or another, every mother has had a serious argument with her son or daughter. The anger and resentment that follows this argument builds way out of proportion to the situation that caused the argument. Hearts are bruised and battered, and hurt is a dull ache at the back of the throat. Neither party wants to give up the desire to be right, and often a stalemate is reached. Both parties need to be reminded of the mother-daughter/son relationship and how important it is.

✝ Lord, I argued with my daughter/son. I know I am right. After all, I am the mother here. Why is it so difficult to get through these situations? They seem to come up repeatedly, and the anger and resentment seem to escalate each time. It hurts my heart. I ask for healing for both of us. Please lift the heaviness from our hearts and diffuse the hurt and resentment that blocks the love and caring that is the bedrock of our relationship. Let me remember that although I feel that I am right, I need to be more open when talking with my child. Please shine your grace on me that I will make the first move to reconcile our differences. Let us forgive one another for the harsh words we used and agree to disagree. Teach us both that we are not always right, and that it is okay to be wrong. Remind us that we are family, and that we must always be here for one another. Moreover, let us learn to use words that are less hurtful, so we can make this journey through life in a close, loving relationship. Amen.

Dealing with a Teenage Child

The teenage years are difficult for both parents and children. There is so much going on in a child's body and mind, and they are anxious to demonstrate how grown up they are through many displays of independence. However, they are still prone to lapses in good judgment.

One area where this occurs is in the picking of friends and activities. How does a parent keep a child on a path to success and happiness without being totally overbearing and dictatorial? How does a parent remain open to the needs of the child, but maintain parental control over situations that could have adverse affects? It is like walking the high wire at the circus. There is a lot of skill needed and it can be beautiful to watch, but if a mistake is made, it is a big fall with great hurt.

Lord, I feel like I am the star of the high-wire act in the circus, and my footing is unstable. I could "blow" this act at any moment. My child is growing up and has let me know through conversations and actions, that he/she is ready to demonstrate independence. This is a new experience for me. I am used to nurturing and caring for this child and making all the decisions. More importantly, I feel that this loved child of mine is on a path to destruction. I look at the friends he/she is making and the people he/she is growing close to, and I can see that some of these individuals are less than stellar in their actions. They skip school, they have no ambition, they drink, they do drugs, they carry guns, or they are what in my day we called "wild."

Please give me the faith, strength, and perseverance to get through this stage of our lives. Help me provide the guidance needed to make sure my child grows up to be a good person. Let me approach my dealings with this child in a manner that he/she will accept, or at least listen to. It may take time—probably more time than I would prefer, but I thank you for the blessing of your grace and the blessing of having such a loving and supportive husband. I put our lives in your hands, knowing that through prayer and faith I can make it through this. Be with me during these troubling times and be with and watch over my child. This I pray in your name. Amen.

Dealing with Drugs

Some people get hooked on drugs, some people don't. For those who do, it is an unbelievable roller coaster ride. It may be fun at the start, but it is a relief when it's over and you get off. The trip is one that is never forgotten. People are hurt, relationships are destroyed, parents and children are deeply affected. How does the woman feel, who has overcome an issue with drugs? What does she say in her prayers?

Lord, thank you that you are in my life and have turned it around. Many years ago, I fell into a terrible drug addiction. One night it was so bad that I prayed to you to let me go to sleep and allow my heart to stop so you could take me away from this world. I no longer wanted to be this person, this addict. What happened to me? I thought I was doing okay, and even though I had a child with a cocaine addict, I had never tried it. As a matter of fact, I ended the relationship because of the drugs.

Then one day someone offered me a line of cocaine and I really wanted to know what made my rival so great. I wanted to know what I was missing. I found out that what I was missing was the need for more. I was missing the money to cover my habit. What I had was watery eyes, an itch for more and more drugs, the inability to make eye contact with anyone, and the realization that I was spiraling out of control.

I was not aware of the phrase, "Let go, and let God," nor of the impact it can have on your life. However, you did not let me just go to sleep and never wake up. I felt that you did not answer my prayer.

However, I was lucky. I became a part of a small church group and shared my story with them. A woman spoke up and made me realize that you did answer my prayer. You did let that part of me die. I no longer want anything to do with drugs. I know that you are real, that you answer prayer, and have a plan for my life and the lives of my children. Thank you for the blessings you have poured into my life. I feel as though that woman was an angel you placed in my life to save me. It did. Thank you. Amen.

A Missing Child

Children go missing. Some disappear as young children, some as adults, and many in between. Just read the milk cartons—Have You Seen Me? What do you do when you receive a call that says that your adult child is missing? Are the feelings the same as for a child or are they different? Are the circumstances the same or are they different?

Lord, my child is missing. I just received a call saying that my child has not been seen for weeks. How can this be? I just spoke with him/her several weeks ago, and he sounded and acted fine. He has a history of medical/mental/physical issues, but with the medication he seemed to be doing okay. The police have been notified and are doing what they can.

It is more difficult with an adult child. He could have decided to get away from it all—from people and surroundings. He could have decided to take a break for a while, not telling anyone where he was going so as not be bothered.

But something is wrong. I feel it in my gut. His cell phone service has been cancelled and his phone has been disconnected. His internet service has been stopped. What has happened?

My plan is to leave my job, go to the area that my child was last seen, speak with as many people as possible that may have been in contact with him, and search for him myself. This is my child—and your child, a child of God. Be with me as I start this arduous search. Let me find this child of mine whom I love so much, and please may he be physically unharmed. Enable me to bring him home and guide him in faith so he will trust you with all areas of his life. Amen.

A Full Plate

We are so busy with work, family, commitments, and friends that often we are overwhelmed with things that must be done. It feels like life is coming at us from all directions at once. If we get one thing done, it seems that there are at least five more that need to be completed. Often we get so mired down that we cannot do anything, and the problem multiplies. How do we deal with all of this?

Lord, my plate is full to overflowing. How did I lose control of so many things all at once? Things are not being completed at work and at home. I feel that I am neglecting my friends, my family, my pets, and my home. Sometimes things seem so piled up, I can't do anything. Then there is just more to do. It is really getting me down. I am embarrassed that my life has fallen into such a shambles.

Matthew 11:28 says, "Come unto me, all ye that labour and are heavy laden, and I will give you rest." Lift me up and bring me the rest that I need. Guide me in the steps I need to follow to take control of my life and to organize the things I need to do. Help me set priorities and eliminate those things that can be left undone. Show me how to create balance in my life so I am comfortable with what I am accomplishing and have quality time to spend connecting with family and friends. Let me remember that sometimes I have to put myself first. Lead me in my life plan so I find contentment and those around me can benefit from it. Amen.

Drunk Drivers

Drunk drivers continue to take a growing toll on the world and the people in it. They hurt people, they maim people, they scar people, and in some cases, they kill people. Anyone who has survived an incident involving a drunk driver has required a great deal of time to adjust to the outcome of that chance meeting. The person who survives the encounter needs a great deal of healing, both physically and emotionally. The people whose lives are shattered by the loss of a loved one deal with the deepest grief imaginable. How do they do it?

Drunk Driver—Personal Loss

Lord, help me. I've lost a limb (or the ability to walk, talk, etc.). How am I going to survive this? Life was good and I was handling the speed bumps pretty well until now. I'm not sure I can get over this one. I feel like my life has been shattered—my body certainly has. The physical and emotional pain is like nothing I have ever experienced.

Give me strength to do what is needed to recover my body and reclaim my life, no matter how much pain or how many setbacks I have to endure. Let me look to you, knowing that faith will see me through the days and weeks of recovery ahead of me. Psalm 145:20 says, "The Lord preserveth all them that love him." I pray that you will preserve me and lift me up. Show me where this tragedy will take me in my life. Amen

Drunk Driver—Loss of a Loved One

Lord, my (husband, son, daughter, friend) is gone—killed by a drunk driver who, of course, walked away unscathed. The pain in my heart is unbearable. I am falling into a depression that could swallow me, but it looks so comforting right now. My other (children, friends, or family) are broken. Some are inconsolable. I feel that I need to be there for them, but I barely have the strength for myself.

Hebrews 13:6 says, "The Lord is my helper, and I will not fear what man shall do unto me." Let me not be afraid. I ask for your help, your healing, and your guidance. What has been done to me by another is a tragedy. I will miss all the happy times and smiles we shared. When I think of him/her, all I do is cry. Shine your grace upon me that I will be able to survive this loss, be there for others, and learn to remember the good times. May I realize the blessing that was mine, even if only for a brief time. Amen.

Illness of an Adult Child

Children get sick. They have colds, flu, and any other number of ailments. They skin their knees and break their bones. We see them through and help them heal. What happens when your adult daughter with a child of her own becomes so ill she needs to have full time nursing care? What other areas of your life does it affect? What are your feelings and what are your fears?

Lord, my daughter was so ill they told me she might die. She is a mother with a child of her own and this illness resulted in the miscarriage of another child she was carrying. They are my grandchildren.

Thank you, God, that she is out of the hospital. Thank you that she is alive. Grant me strength and wisdom to help us all through what I am told will be a long and tough recovery. My whole life feels like it has been turned upside down. I am missing work, but not as much as I thought I would have to miss. I have no social life.

All of my time is spent taking care of my child or my grandchild, and trying to lift them up from the depression each of them is battling. I don't begrudge them that at all. I love them with all my heart, and there is nothing I wouldn't do to pull them through this. But it is strange to change your child's diaper, and their child's diaper. It's difficult to come to grips with a condition that requires me to bathe my child and my grandchild, and feed my child and my grandchild. Technically, I have two infants. My tears are silent (or at least seen by few if any) but copious. I am scared and I am sad. Give me all the skills a mother needs (in duplicate) and all the love I need to give to them. Give me strength through your loving grace and give that same strength and more to my daughter. Send her healing so that she may be there to share all the good and fun things in life that mothers and daughters share—with me and with her daughter. This I pray in your name. Amen.

Being an Alcoholic

"Hello, my name is _____ and I am an alcoholic."

That's how people introduce themselves at an Alcoholics Anonymous (AA) meeting. It is not the way we usually meet an alcoholic or know if someone is an alcoholic. They will not usually tell us. There are over two million members in AA. What is it like for the person who cannot stop drinking, or who cannot have just one drink? What weighs on their hearts and minds?

Lord, I am an alcoholic. Most times I don't mention that to friends or loved ones. I did once. It was at a time when I was going to AA meetings and getting help. Then I fell off the wagon—again. I seem to do so well for periods of time, some long, some not so long. Then out of the blue, I want a drink. No, I need a drink. Where does that come from and why does it keep bugging me? I do well and then I drink, and drink, and drink. I'm back in oblivion and have no memory of many of the things that happened while I was drinking. My family has given up on me and I don't have my children with me. I miss them so much. They are my life, but so is alcohol. It takes away my self-confidence. I feel unfit to raise my children and incapable of holding down a job.

Lord, be with me. Help me find the strength to admit that I have a problem and seek out people who will support me and help me in my efforts to beat this demon. Enable me to go to the meetings and embrace the Twelve-Step program and succeed. If faith can move mountains, let me see that it can bring me back to what most people describe as a normal life, one that keeps me close to my children, my family, my friends, and most importantly, my God. Give me a life that keeps me far, far away from alcohol forever. This I pray in your name. Amen.

Budget Problems

At one time or another most everyone experiences some sort of problem budgeting their money—trying to stretch what they earn to cover what they need to pay. It may be a case where you are a little short and have to pay the minimum on a bill that is due. It may be a situation where there is so little money that something is not going to be paid at all. How do you handle the pressure and satisfy everyone who wants a piece of your cash?

Lord, what has happened to me? More specifically, what has happened to my money? I am so short of cash that I am not sure how I am going to pay my bills. This is terrifying to me! Where will this lead it if keeps up? I could lose my home or my car. I could end up being unable to feed myself or my family. I could end up in court or in jail for failure to pay my bills. I don't understand how this got so out of hand. Please sit beside me as I go over these numbers. Be with me as I decide how best to get a better handle on my money. I need to write down where I am spending money and what I am buying with that money.

Show me how to be wise and cut out unnecessary expenses—maybe take both breakfast and lunch to work, eat out less, don't buy that book or piece of clothing, do more comparison shopping. Guide me as I do all I can to get back on track. Help me spend less and save more, or at least have enough to pay my bills. Lead me toward financial security so I may in turn help others and give back to you. Amen.

Cleaning Out the Closet

Closets have a tendency to get full or cluttered, or both. So from time to time you just have to do something to get them straightened out. The size of this chore depends on the size of the closet and the amount of clutter, but it is not something most people look forward to doing. What thoughts run through your mind as you contemplate tackling this task?

L ord, I need to clean out this closet, and I can think of at least a hundred other things I would rather do. The closet is a mess with shoes all over the place and clothes crammed in every which way. I get frustrated when I am trying to find something to wear and the shoes to wear with the outfit. Some of the clothes fit and some don't. I should get rid of the ones that don't fit, but what if I end up needing that size again? I can't just go out and buy a whole new wardrobe.

Walk into the darkness of that closet with me. Help me do what needs to be done to get that closet organized, in the hope that it will affect other parts of my life in addition to my overall appearance. May I remember that there are people in great need of clothes and I have many that I can't even wear. Let me share what I see as a problem (too many clothes that don't fit) with someone who will see it as a blessing (having any clothes to wear). Let cleaning out that closet be the first step on the way to cleaning up other parts of my life. As my life is cleansed, so let my heart be cleansed. Let it be more open and have more space for you and for the wondrous things you have in store for me. Amen.

I Have an Attitude

At one time or another we all have days when the world overtakes us and we develop an attitude— a negative one at that. We say things we shouldn't say. We do things we shouldn't do. We are not very nice to people. How do we let that happen, and when it does, what should we do about it?

Lord, this has been such a bad day. Did I get up on the wrong side of the bed or did something else cause the horrible mood I was in all day? I really had an attitude. I was driving aggressively to get to work and once I got there, I was not very nice to anyone. I was sure I was right about everything and they were not right about anything. I wasn't very diplomatic in the way I handled conversations with them.

Please help me avoid letting an attitude get the better of me. Remind me that I may not always be right. May I learn that someone else may have a different perspective and it may be right too. Enable me to be more open to the ideas and opinions of others. May I remember to practice the Golden Rule and do to unto others as they would do unto me. Before I say or do something, may I ask myself if it is something I would say or do to friends or family. Be with me and enable me to grow in character. This I pray in your name. Amen.

Menopause

Which is worse—PMS or Menopause? Who knows? Both affect women in different ways and not usually for the better. Both have to do with the hormonal levels in our bodies. Some individuals have little or no problems with either one, and some people have acute problems with either one or both. In most cases, a physician's involvement is necessary at some point. How do you deal with the onset of the physical and mental changes brought about by the onset of menopause?

Lord, either this situation is nuts or I am. I'm glad that I am alive and have been for so long, but parts of this aging process are tough. Like this menopause thing. One moment I am fine and the next minute I am in tears, for absolutely no reason. My body thermostat is totally dysfunctional! First I am freezing and then I am so hot I'm in a sweat. It makes getting a good night's sleep extremely difficult—pulling the covers on, throwing the covers off—and the effects of the disrupted sleep are taking an affect on me and all of those around me. It certainly takes a toll on your sex life.

Help me to realize that I'm fortunate to have reached this point in my life; many women don't. Let me remember that with all the breakthroughs in medicine, there is a lot more that can be done to make me more comfortable with this menopause phase of my life. Let me open up and talk with friends and physicians and learn to deal with what is happening to my body. Remind me to celebrate no more periods, no more fears of pregnancy, and no more emergency trips to the drug store for sanitary products! Lead me gracefully so that I may be an example to others. Amen.

Being Diagnosed with Cancer

More and more people are being diagnosed with cancer of one sort or another. Perhaps it is from the lifestyle they have lead, or the vices (weaknesses) they have had, or maybe it just happens. The reactions of the patient, the patient's friends, and the patient's family are almost always shock and disbelief. The thoughts that go through their minds are similar but different. The following prayer comes from Colleen Wallace, a friend who passed away in 2007.

Lord, I feel like I have been hit by a bolt of lightning. I was diagnosed with cancer. I have gone from skipping through life with a great job, a busy family, and doing lots of extra meaningless things, to a world of no job, no hair, and worse yet—no eyelashes and no independence. For months I have been reeling.

Help me to stand up and begin to appreciate everything, and I mean everything. May I draw my children and grandchildren closer to me as well as my friends. May I start to plant flowers, travel, delight in each day, and to interact with other cancer patients and survivors. May I read all I can about new treatments and options. Enable me to laugh more, cry more, and not listen to the trivial gripes and complaints of others. Remind me again that it is good to be alive and looking forward to each day. No matter how many more of them I have left, may I make the most of each of them. Help me live each day and enjoy each minute! Amen.

Dealing with Aging

The aging process is a unique experience for everyone. It affects everyone differently or at least at different times. There are physical changes and mental changes, which lead to a number of emotional changes. Jokes are made about aging all the time and we laugh at them. However, when we are going through some of the issues, it is not so much a laughing matter. What are some of the things that we experience, and how do we deal with them?

Lord, this aging process is terrifying. I've always felt pretty comfortable and organized with getting older, but I've reached an age where the process is unstable. I never know what is going to happen or how I am going to perceive or react to one thing or another from day to day. Sometimes I can't remember where I have put things. Sometimes I can't remember why I got up or went into another room. I certainly don't seem to have the stamina, energy, or dexterity that I did when I was in my twenties and thirties. I'm developing aches and pains that either won't go away at all, or leave in their own merry time. I look in the mirror and wonder, "Where did all those wrinkles and sagging come from? They weren't there yesterday!"

Help me realize that I am like everyone else, all creatures in your wonderful world. We all get older, and we all show the signs and symptoms of doing so. May I realize that my diet and exercise (or lack of them) may help in the process (or not), but they won't stop the process. Help me to learn to grow old gracefully, slowing down when I have to, taking notes when I need to, making lists when it is necessary, and accepting the process as a blessing. How fortunate I am that I have reached this age; many of my friends never did. I have enjoyed so many experiences over the years. How blessed I have been with friends and family every step of the way. Give me strength and may my faith remain strong as I get ever and ever older. Amen.

How do Hobbies become so Political?

Many people have some type of hobby, many of which are competitive, such as a sport or a competition. At some point disagreements arise, politics enter into the scene, and people get angry and hurt. How do things get so out of hand and so political, and what do we do when it happens?

Lord, you know that I love my hobby. I spend a lot of my non-working time participating in it. I spend a lot of money doing it, too. I have enjoyed the people and the competitive nature and have had the good fortune to do well a time or two. All of a sudden someone questioned my adherence to the rules and said that I cheated. They didn't use that word, but that is what they meant. I feel like they questioned my ethics and my integrity, and I am really hurt and even more angry. I love my hobby, and I am an honest person. I've won and I've lost, but I try to play by the rules. I just can't get past these feelings of total betrayal. This person was supposed to be my friend.

Be with me and enable me to cool off and calm down. Help me remember that even though someone said something hurtful that I feel is totally untrue, I have to get past it. I know in my heart that I did not purposely do anything wrong or try to jeopardize the outcome of the event. May I be true to myself, and forgive the person who harmed me with words. Enable me to continue with my hobby, being even more aware of what I do and how I do it. This I pray in your name. Amen.

Not being Selected for a Certain Job

Each of us has applied for a job sometime during our life. It may have been a part-time job while we were in school. It may have been a part-time or full-time job after we completed our education, or maybe we were trying to change jobs. Sometimes we didn't get that job. Maybe we did not get several jobs we applied for, either during a specific job-hunting period or over a longer period in our lives. Emotionally it took a toll on us. The following is a prayer to help us understand and deal with not being selected for a certain job.

Lord, I did not get that job, and I wanted it so badly. I mean, I am perfect for that job. I can do it. I thought the interview went really well and that I would be the chosen candidate. I am really quite upset and emotionally I am dealing with feelings of inadequacy. Maybe I am not as good as I think I am. Help me to remember the words of an old, old song and "lift myself up, dust myself off, and start all over again." The company thought enough of my resume and skills to talk with me. Maybe they had already picked a candidate for the position. That does not mean I could not have done the job or that I am not qualified. Let me look to you for faith. Let me look back through my resume and recall my strengths and all that I can bring to a job. Lead me to a job that takes advantage of my skills and offers me an opportunity to grow—a job that leads me on the path of life that you want me to take. This I pray in your name. Amen.

You don't Like your Job

Too many people stay in jobs they don't like. They do it for any number of reasons. Every day they go to work and it is hard work, because they don't like what they are doing, or they don't like their boss, or they just don't like working. How can they make more of their life and touch others to make more of theirs?

Lord, I hate my job. I know hate is a strong word, but I really do hate it. It's not fun. It's drudgery. Getting up in the morning is a struggle. The motivation to start working when I get to the office takes all that I have, and some mornings it takes hours! I want to do more. I want to work for and with people I respect and get along with and can work with as a team. I'm tired of all the backbiting and holding back of information. But I need a job. I need the benefits. I need the paycheck.

Give me the will to learn more about myself and what it is I really want to do. Let me look at my skills and recognize my strengths. And let me also look at those areas where I am not as strong and figure out what I need to do (classes, reading, mentoring,etc.) to acquire the skills to get into a job with a company where I can grow and learn, and where I can feel that I have accomplished something good every day when I walk out the door.

I don't want to just work. I want a career or a calling. I want to wake up in the morning excited about everything the day will bring my way. Hold me up, help me persevere, and lead me to success. This I pray in your name. Amen.

Frustration with Co-workers

Each of us thinks differently and each of us reacts differently. Each of us has our own work ethic, some stronger than others. So what happens when we all come together in a work environment? Often opinions get in the way and tempers flare. We get frustrated with our co-workers, sometimes for valid reasons, sometimes for not such valid reasons. So what do we do, and how do we feel, and how do we better ourselves?

✝ Lord, I am so frustrated with my co-worker (or co-workers). I feel like I am the only one doing any work around here. What's the deal? I'm swamped with work, and although they say they are so-o-o-o busy, they certainly seem to be wasting a lot of time talking on the phone, playing computer games, talking with people, or being away from their desks. At the end of the year, they will get the same raise that I get—the old across-the-board percentage. I just don't feel like that is fair. I get so down and discouraged, and sometimes just plain frustrated and angry! Please be with me. If I *am* the only one doing any work, then let me take pride in the work that I do and realize that I am contributing to the success of my organization. Let me celebrate my successes, whether anyone else does or not. Remind me that I am blessed to have a job and that I get a raise at all. Help me remember that I am the one who is benefitting from having the opportunity to work on these tasks. I have a chance to accomplish something, learn something, and feel good when I go home at night, knowing that I've done what was expected of me. Let me concentrate more on how to make my job better, maybe even easier, and concentrate less and gripe less about what others are not doing. If I do that I can grow, and if I can set an example for others, maybe they can grow too. Amen.

When a Consultant is Hired to Do Your Job

Often organizations will hire a consultant to help with a project, even though there is a knowledgeable staff person who could or should be heading up the work. The purpose in many cases is to ensure that there are sufficient staff and sufficient knowledge to accomplish the project, particularly if it is a major initiative. However, the consultant takes total charge, and the staff person is often left to wonder what her role is. How does the staff person feel, and how does she handle this in a professional manner resulting in a positive outcome?

Lord, I feel like I just lost my job, but I am still employed. The organization brought in a consultant to work with me, but the consultant is running over me. I have always taken pride in the work I do and in my knowledge of what I am doing. I understand that we are having a major meeting, and an outside consultant can provide expertise on how to organize a meeting of that magnitude. However, I have a good grasp of the knowledge of the topic of the meeting, and the consultant doesn't seem to feel that some key content is important. He is emphasizing the more commercial aspect of the meeting.

Please give me patience and persistence in getting my points across. Lord, help me be courteously adept at making sure that the content that is so important (at least in my opinion) is not only included, but also presented in an informative and exciting manner. In so doing, give me back my self-confidence in the job that I am responsible for, and a sense of pride in doing that job well. This I pray in your name. Amen.

The Loss of a Job

At one time or another we may experience the loss of a job. This may be due to downsizing, restructuring, or being let go for other reasons. Even if we had an idea or actually knew this was going to happen, it still comes as a shock. We now have many decisions to make and many aspects of our lives to reevaluate. We need to develop a plan of action and move forward with our lives.

✝ Lord. I lost my job today. I knew (or didn't know) it was coming, and it was really a shock. I need a job. I have to pay my mortgage and my bills, and other living expenses. What am I going to do? How am I going to explain this to my friends and family? I am embarrassed. I feel like a failure. Why do I feel this way? I worked hard, I was always on time, I even stayed late when it was necessary. My boss gave me good reviews and raises. How did this happen? Let me look to you for strength. Let me remember that when I was hired it was because someone saw in me the skills and abilities they needed for the success of their company or department. They believed in me and the talents I brought to their organization. So I have skills and abilities. I even have education!

Help me go out and find another job. That's not always easy, so maybe I will have to work part time or as a temporary employee. That seems like a step down in my mind, but I ask that you help me remember that you have a plan for my life and this is all part of that plan. This may be your way of showing me what you need me to do. This may be the opportunity I need to acquire additional skills, meet new people, and find new opportunities. Perhaps this is when I will realize that I have skills I was not really aware of that will be the springboard to an even better job than I had. May I trust in you to watch over me as I move forward in my life. Enable me to find success, and in so doing be successful in fulfilling your plan for my life. This I pray in your name. Amen.

My Water Pipes Broke!

Do you know how expensive it can be when your water pipes break, not to mention the overall inconvenience? How do you get them fixed, where does the money come from, and whom do you call? Whether in an apartment, condo, townhouse, or single family home, broken pipes are a calamity!

✝   Lord, what a mess! My water pipes broke! I came home and there was a note on the door that my water has been turned off. I talked with the insurance company and they will not pay for the repairs. I talked with the homeowners association and they won't pay for them. I talked with the utility company and they won't pay for them, either. You've got to be kidding! I'm told that this will cost thousands of dollars and I have to pay for all of it, and my water will not be turned on until it is fixed. I don't have thousands of dollars. What am I going to do?

Please be with me and help me maintain some calm during this storm. Help me talk with friends, neighbors, and other associates and ask their advice, and help me listen to that advice. Help me determine what financial options I have, or can create, to pay for this. Please send answers quickly so I might have this resolved as soon as possible. I certainly cannot afford to stay in a hotel and I really need bathroom facilities and the ability to shower. Enable my faith and my determination to be strong. Through prayer, may I seek and find the answers I need to restore my home to its original working order. Help me find the money, and help me realize that it will be money well spent on what is certainly a life necessity. Amen.

My House Burned Down (or Up)

What a roller-coaster ride you take when your
home is lost to a fire! You are elated that you're alive,
and devastated that you have lost everything. How
do you feel about the losses and the recovery? How
do you deal with the insurance company minutia
and other tasks that must be handled? How do you
find comfort living in temporary housing?

✝ Lord, my God, my house is gone! It went up in flames and smoke, and I was in it. Thank you that we escaped safely and with minimal harm from smoke inhalation. Thank you that we are alive!

The aftermath is as horrible as the fire. Dealing with the insurance company, stopping the paper, the electricity, and everything else, is so time-consuming! Trying to find a place to live, even with help, takes more time than I would have thought. Having to look at the shell of my home of so many years hurts so badly, and sifting through my belongings to see if anything is salvageable is heart-wrenching. All my stuff!

Please help me remember that it was just "stuff" and it can be replaced. Help me learn to appreciate the fact that I was fortunate to have accumulated such wealth and possessions. Help me move forward with a stronger sense of appreciation for what I have and for what I will have. May I use my possessions wisely and share my good fortune with others. Keep me calm as I transition to a new home, and to a new life. May I sing your praises that I am alive and have been given more time to do what it is that will most benefit your kingdom. Amen.

The Loss of a Friend due to Changes in Lifestyles

As young children, we have neighborhood and/or family playmates. During the school years we develop close relationships with classmates. When we go into the work world, our friends tend to be our peers, others in the same profession, bosses (sometimes), perhaps customers, and, of course, neighbors. As we make these transitions, we lose some friends and make others. This may be due to the development of other interests or activities, or perhaps because of marriage, children, or physical moves. In some cases it occurs because one or the other of us has in some way hurt the other person deeply. Sometimes we are actually relieved at the loss of a friend who has chosen activities that we cannot accept, but in other cases we feel an empty place within us at the loss of the friend. Let's pray about loss and friends.

Lord, it has dawned on me that I lost a friend. We just drifted apart (he or she moved away; I can't abide their actions; or I hurt them or they hurt me). I feel an empty space in my heart. I thought that we would be life-long friends and this would not be a fair-weather friendship, and now it's gone. Whether for good or bad, something that was important to me and played a big part in my life is no longer there. Let me always remember that I am blessed and have been blessed with the gift of friendship. At each step in my life you have provided a person or persons to be my friend, to support me in what I am doing and what I am dealing with at any particular time.

May I remember the e-mail that circulated many times saying that a person comes into your life for a reason, a season, or a lifetime. Give me the perspective to put this person into one of those categories, and give thanks for the friendship we shared. Help me move on with my life knowing there will be other friendships and knowing that I have friends in each category—and they are there for a purpose. Remind me of what I read in a book that said God puts friends in our lives as a reminder that he is thinking of us. May I be glad that you watch so closely over me. Amen.

The Loss of a Friend through Death from Illness

The loss of a friend through death can occur at any time in our lives. This particular prayer will speak to what it is like to lose a friend as an adult—something most women will experience. When this begins to happen, I recall a quote of my father's, "This is a terrible time of life." He was speaking of the fact that as he got older, more and more of his friends passed away and he explained how difficult it was to deal with the losses. Perhaps the following prayer will help cope with the losses we experience.

Lord, I miss (this person) so much. I can't believe she/he is gone. In this case I knew it was expected; she/he had been ill for such a long time, fighting such a valiant fight. Still again, she/he is gone.

I pray that you bless their soul and be with their family during this time of loss. May they look to you for strength through faith. And be with me. Help me to look back and remember the wonderful times we spent together. May I celebrate the fabulous adventures we shared. Remind me again and again that she/he is no longer suffering or fighting for her/his life on this earth, and that she/he is with you in heaven, dancing with the angels and singing songs of praise. May she/he live in my heart, and come back to visit in my mind. I ask you again to bless her/his soul, and I ask that you bless me, too. Amen.

Suicide

In the United States someone commits suicide every sixteen minutes. Each suicide ultimately affects at least six other people. If someone you know is suicidal what do you do? How do you deal with the fact that someone you know has committed suicide? What feelings are racing through your mind? How do you process what happened and help others to process it too?

✝ Lord, I am so devastated. My (friend, partner, spouse, relative) committed suicide. I had felt for some time that she was unhappy or overly worried or something. I knew that at times she felt overwhelmed by the circumstances of her life. I feel guilty and blame myself. I should have been more open and talked with her about suicide. I should have been non-judgmental when I did talk with her. I should have listened more, and I should have listened more carefully. I should have talked with crisis intervention agencies or recommended that they talk to her. I hurt so much.

I have learned a lot by going through these last few days. The affect on me, on her friends, and on her family is one of the saddest experiences I have ever had. Lift these feelings of guilt and self-blame from my shoulders. Help me continue to learn. Help me continue to heal and help others to heal. May I remember that my (friend, partner, spouse, relative) is no longer in pain; the anguish is gone. She has no more worries. Shine your grace down upon me and upon all who were touched by this loss and may it heal our hurt. This I pray in your name. Amen.

An Abusive Relationship

If we have not been in an abusive relationship, we probably know someone who has. Whether the abuse is physical or emotional, the signs are often hard to see, but the symptoms become clear as time passes. Some people in these relationships cannot find the strength to escape them, and the abuse takes a terrible (and sometimes fatal) toll, not only on them, but also on their family and friends. What goes through a woman's mind when she is aware of the abuse?

Lord, help me. He has hurt me so much. I've reached a point where I feel that I deserve what he does to me. I feel that I am not worthy of more. He has made me feel that this is my fault, that I have brought it on myself and I deserve it. I've tried to leave but he threatens me and he threatens our children. I can't let him harm my children.

My family and friends tell me to get out of this relationship and go start a new life. They just don't understand. I have been made to feel that I can't even run a household or raise children well—what can I do in a new life—fail again?

Father God, please be with me. Bring me strength through faith. Help me look to you for answers. Help me find what you have planned for me to do with my life, and figure out how to carry out your plan. Please keep my friends and family close to me (as close as they can be in the circumstances), so I know that someone cares about me and that someone is there to remind me of your love for me.

Isaiah 25:8 says, "The Lord God will wipe away tears from off all faces." Wipe away my tears. Be with me and lead me in a direction that will release me from this pain and suffering. This I pray in your name. Amen.

Disappearance of a Spouse

Husbands may disappear for a few hours, or a day sometimes. Usually they come back and it's not that they actually disappeared; they just took a trip or a break or whatever. What does a woman feel when her husband truly does disappear? What thoughts go through her head, and how does she handle the conflicting emotions raging within her? How does she manage to keep it together and move forward?

✝   Lord, my husband disappeared—eleven months ago. I mean it's not like he went to the club to shoot a couple rounds of golf or the local bar to have a few drinks. He's gone! I'm assuming he is not with another woman, because by now I feel that I would have had a message from him wanting a divorce.

These last months have been brutal on me. I was so blown away when I came home eleven months ago and he and the car were gone, and he never called or came back. He was my high school sweetheart and we have been married for almost ten years. What happened? Is he dead or alive? If he is alive, is he okay? Why doesn't he contact me? I've been beside myself with worry. The police have found nothing.

I am calmer than I was eleven months ago, thanks to you. My faith has provided the strength I have needed to battle my way through this mire in my life. Thank you that I am still alive, that I have a job, and that I can take care of myself pretty well. Thank you that we never had children. This would have been so much harder to deal with had there been children. And what would I tell them?

Lord, please stay with me. I feel that I am walking through the valley of darkness. Find my husband and let us figure out what we are doing and where we are going. Please may he be okay. No matter what happens, may I depend on the support of my faith and your grace to help me not only move forward with my life, but to excel at whatever it is that I do. Amen.

The Loss of a Spouse through Divorce (no children)

How does a woman feel when her husband leaves her? Some may actually be relieved, but most are extremely upset. Divorce is difficult for everyone, even those who feel it is what they want and believe they have found something better than what they had. There are still heartstrings attached, no matter what the circumstances. There are feelings of inadequacy, hurt, possibly betrayal, and sometimes guilt. How do you continue down life's path?

Lord, he left me. He just said that he did not want to be married anymore. I knew something was wrong, but I could not get him to talk about it. He will not even go to counseling. Help me wrap my mind around the fact that this marriage is over, no matter how much I want it to continue. I feel like I've lost everything. We have to sell the house as part of the settlement and I have to find somewhere else to live. Many of the people we socialize with are perplexed and cannot figure out who to invite where and how to do it. Some of them only do couples, so I know where that leaves me. For as long as I was single, I would not have thought it would be so hard to adjust to not being married.

I loved being married and doing things together. We had such similar tastes, likes, and dislikes. It was a lot of fun. Sometimes things were difficult, but not really bad.

Help me get past this speed bump in my life. Help me realize that he loved me, even if he doesn't anymore. Help me hang on to the good times and not dwell on the bad ones. Help me take the initiative to talk with someone who can help me. May I remember that you are always there to watch over me, and that you will get me past this speed bump without letting it be a head-on collision. Keep me mindful of the fact that you love me and are always there to pick me up when I fall. I turn to you for strength through faith, knowing you will place me on the path that is best for your plan for my life. God, be with me on this difficult journey. This I pray in your name. Amen.

.

The Loss of a Spouse through Death

Husbands die. Some die in accidents, some at war, some through illness, and some from nothing more than old age. Whether you knew he would or might die, you weren't ready. Whether you have been with that spouse for a short time or a very long time, the loss is overwhelming. Someone who was a part of every aspect of your life is gone. The someone special you talked with and shared your hopes and dreams with is no longer there to listen and to share. How do you survive the grieving process?

✞ Lord, he died. I'm just lost. He was my husband and I loved him. We had such grand times together. Even the rough times were easy to look back on once we got past them. They even brought a laugh or two from time to time. I so wish he was still here. I need him. My whole life routine is built around the life we had together. When to work, when to play, when to eat, when to sleep—they were all a joint effort, even if I did think I was in control of the whole routine. Now it is just me, and I can't get into any routine. I feel like I have been drugged. I cannot eat, I do not sleep, and any idea of playing or socializing is the farthest thing from my mind. I feel like I am drowning in my grief.

Lift me up, Lord. Help me learn to remember and celebrate the wonderful times we had without disintegrating into tears. Give me back my smile and my enthusiasm to live. Show me that I can go out and play an active part in the world through the talents you have given me to share. I will never forget him, but I need you to help me plan a future and live it with enthusiasm. If I show the world that I can do it, then maybe I can help someone else realize that they can do it too. Be with me as I move forward with every aspect of my life. Amen.

Death of Parents

If we live long enough, we all lose our parents to death. If we have siblings, they can either create a support line or perhaps express their feelings in less than loving terms. If we are an only child, the loss can be felt more deeply because there are no siblings. Once we have lost both of our parents, the feelings of children with or without siblings can be very similar. What goes through the minds of women when they no longer have parents?

Lord, as of today both of my parents have died. I knew they would die; that is a fact of life. I'm an orphan and that is such a strange feeling. Oh, the things we take for granted! Even though I knew they would die, a part of me thought they would always be here. This is more traumatic than I would have ever anticipated. When you lose your parents, you lose your support, not just your support system. I feel unbalanced. I have always displayed my independence (isn't that always difficult for parents to adjust to?), but I now realize how dependent I was on their unconditional love and their unending support. They were always there for me, through the good, the bad, and the ugly. I know that time will heal my hurting heart. In its place will be a heart and mind that remember the good times they had.

Comfort me, Lord, and help me remember how much they enjoyed their life with its travels, friends, and family. Thank you for the blessings you provided me through my parents, even when I did not always agree with them. May I keep the good times in my heart and share them with my friends and family, creating a legacy that will continue through time. Help me remember what Matthew 5:4 says, "Blessed are they that mourn: for they shall be comforted." This I ask in your name. Amen.

Living Alone

Some women always live alone. Some women end up living alone because of divorce, death, or separation. What is it like not to have a "man around the house" to help with chores, to spend quality time with, to engage in stimulating conversation, and to seduce?

Lord, sometimes I love the fact that I live alone. I can come and go as I wish without asking someone else if it is okay with them. I can make and change whatever plans I want to whenever I want to. I can have breakfast, lunch, or dinner when the mood strikes me, and I can eat whatever appeals to me at the time—whether it's a full meal or not and whether or not it is healthy.

There are other times, however, when I don't like living alone. I want to share a meal and some conversation with someone else. I want to share experiences. I want to bounce ideas off someone and see what they think. I need someone to help me with all the little tasks that I don't know how to do, like changing the shower head, replacing the screens, installing appliances, and all the other "fix it" jobs that pop up. I just need someone to share my life. If your plan includes someone in my life, I will be truly blessed. If it does not, may I realize that, too, may be a blessing. Help me see that I can handle anything that comes up—or at least most of what comes up. Help me learn to luxuriate in the freedoms that living alone offers me. And may I use the gifts you have given me to show others that they can do it too, if the need arises. Amen.

Spending Christmas Alone

It's the holiday season, and you are alone while everyone is with family, friends, or loved ones. You now understand why this time of the year is when the highest incidence of depression occurs. How can you make it through this season with its parties, celebrations, glitz, and gift-giving when you just don't feel like parties, celebrations, glitz, and gift-giving? What can you do to ensure that you don't slip into an abyss of depression and do something that may be detrimental to you or someone else? How do you hang in there and look forward to celebrating another new year?

Lord, I am alone for Christmas and I am feeling very lonely. I have friends, I have faith, and I have a church, but I still feel very lonely. I cannot motivate myself to attend church services, I refuse to send cards, and I feel like I would be perfectly happy just to be alone. But something inside tells me that I am moping, pouting, and being selfish.

Help me realize that no matter what the season, you are with me. Help me forget about the commercialization of Christmas and remember that this is a time for everyone to celebrate the birth of your Son, who came to save us all. May he sit next to me so I can feel His presence and know he is always with me and will watch over me always. Help me celebrate His coming with a prayer, and share that good news with others through prayer and conversations. Even though I feel down, help me spend time with church family and with friends, even if it is very brief, knowing that the interaction will help keep me from slipping into a dark hole. Get me outside, even if it is only long enough to walk around the parking lot or the block. Help me to be glad for the blessings and gifts you have bestowed on me, and may I learn that the best thing I can do is to share those gifts with others. Sharing with others and taking the time to make them the focus of attention will shift the attention from me and put the emphasis on you, which is where it should be. In so doing, lift me up and lighten my heart. This I pray in your name. Amen.

Hip Replacement

More and more people are undergoing surgery for hip replacements. Fortunately, the medical world has vastly improved the processes and successes of this type of surgery. What is it like for the person facing this type of surgery? What are they feeling, and what are their concerns about the surgery and the recovery?

✝ Lord, I need hip replacement surgery. There is no doubt in my mind that my hip is worn out. I am in so much pain—not discomfort, pain—almost constantly. I cannot walk. I can barely sit down, and finding a comfortable position to sleep is almost impossible.

I know that this surgery is being performed more and more and the success rate is extremely high. However, I still have concerns. I will be "out of commission" for several weeks following the surgery and my activities will be limited even longer. What if something goes wrong? What will I do then? I cannot imagine losing my ability to get around, drive a car, and walk through the store or the mall, or even just the neighborhood.

Please lift me up and make me well. Enable my physicians to be magicians. Be with me as I undergo this surgery and carry me quickly through the recovery. Keep me optimistic and determined. May I be the person who beats all the records for a quick and complete recovery. Then may I be the person who encourages others to have the surgery if it is needed and to help alleviate their fears. This I pray in your name. Amen.

Living In a Retirement Community

The number of continuing care retirement communities is on the rise across the country. Many people are moving into them, and often there is a waiting list. Many people have opted to live in these communities, liking the amenities offered and the chance to free themselves of the upkeep on a home. Others would love to stay in their home, but their friends and/or families worry about them. What are the thoughts that go through peoples' minds as they make this lifestyle change? How do they get used to living a more regimented life?

Lord, here I am in this continuing care retirement community. They call it a CCRC in the business. I call it "the county home." Please help me adjust. Let's face it, I came here to die. It is a beautiful "campus," and it is well cared for and groomed. I like the apartment where I live and the view is very nice. It is smaller than my home was and there is no yard, but I guess not having to be out in the blazing sun all day gardening or doing yard work may be a good thing. Meals are provided and there are always nurses available in case they are needed and that is a good thing. If I get to a point where I need daily help, I can move into the assisted living section of the community, and there is an Alzheimer's unit and a nursing home section, too, and that is a good thing.

Help me grow accustomed to having so many people in the dining room. My one at home was not as formal and it was cozier. May I remember that the staff are cooking for lots of people and are not prone to cater to the ways I like my food cooked. I need to be grateful that someone else is doing the cooking and I have several choices at each meal. They do the dishes too, and that is a good thing.

Being here is like living in a small town where everyone knows everyone else's business. If they are talking about me, help me put it in the context that I am a fascinating person or at least the most important person of the day. Smooth the rough edges of my transition. I may be here to die, but help me remember that for each day I am here, I am here to live! This I pray in your name. Amen.